Extra Credit!

Are you ready for a cool school search? Hunt through this puzzle pad and see if you can score the answers to these three activities. If you can, you'll earn an A+ in our book!

Laugh-eteria!

How many of each lunch item can you find?

pizza

hot dog

cupcake

banana

Gym socks!

Can you spot all 6 hidden socks?

Books rule!

Which school tool can you find the most of?

ruler

book

pencil

paper clip

Cover illustrated by Neil Numberman
Silly stories written by Betsy Ochester

Hidden Pictures®

Write a number below each object based on the order in which you find it in the big picture. Then flip the page to create a silly story with the objects!

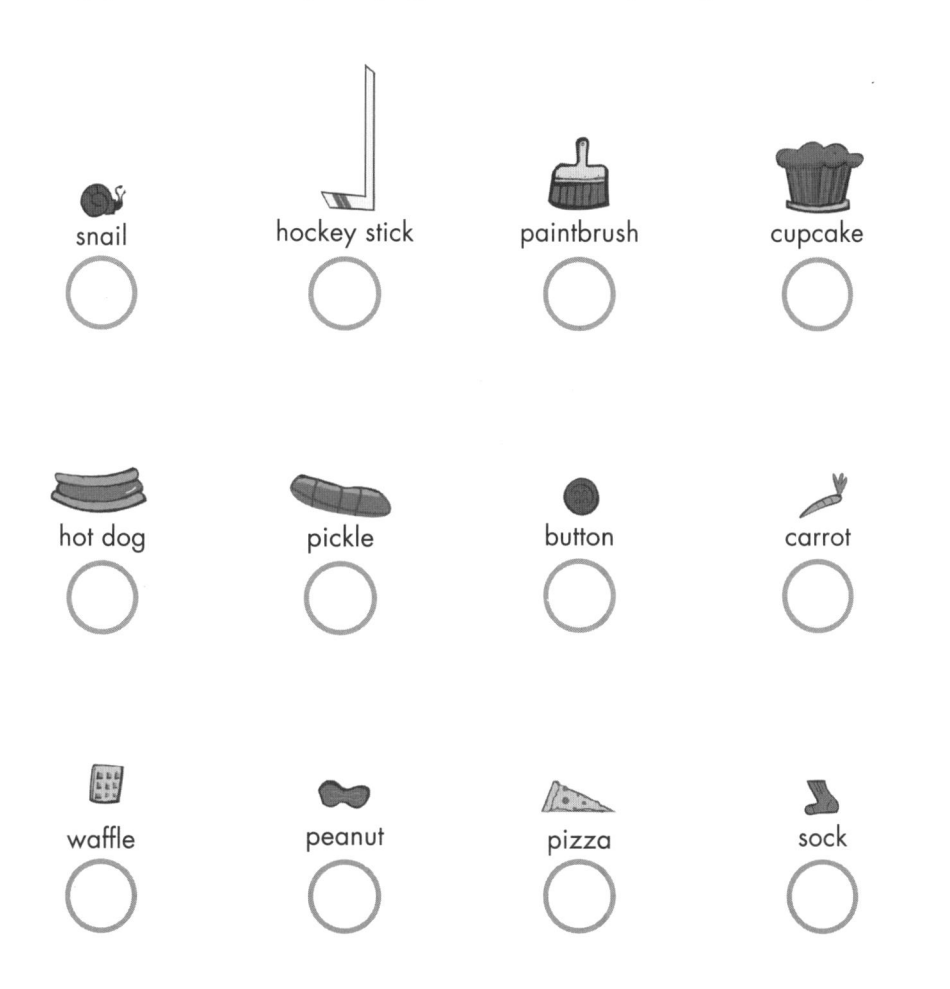

snail

hockey stick

paintbrush

cupcake

hot dog

pickle

button

carrot

waffle

peanut

pizza

sock

BONUS
Can you also find this object?

envelope

Bagpipe Concert

Illustrated by Kevin Rechin

Flip the page!

Bagpipe Concert

Write the object names in the numbered spaces. For example, if you found the waffle first, write "waffle" in the first blank.

Every week our teacher, Ms. _____,
1

brings in a special _____ and we have
2

to write a poem about the experience. Sometimes

that's easy. Like the time a zookeeper brought in

a giant _____ on a leash. Or when
3

a local _____ came to juggle for us
4

wearing a plaid _____. But today's
5

guests were so loud it was hard to think, let alone

write a decent _____. It was The
6

Windy _____ Band, a bagpipe group.
7

I think some members had never picked up their

_____ before. I wanted to put a big
            8

_____ over my ears! But then I got
            9

used to it, and before I knew it, I was tapping my

_____ to the beat. When they finished,
           10

they even let some of the kids in my class try it

out. I got chosen to play! I was so happy, I wrote

this: Remember to squeeze the _____
                                        11

when you play a bagpipe. If you don't, the

_____ will begin to gripe.
           12

Hidden Pictures®

Write a number below each object based on the order in which you find it in the big picture. Then flip the page to create a silly story with the objects!

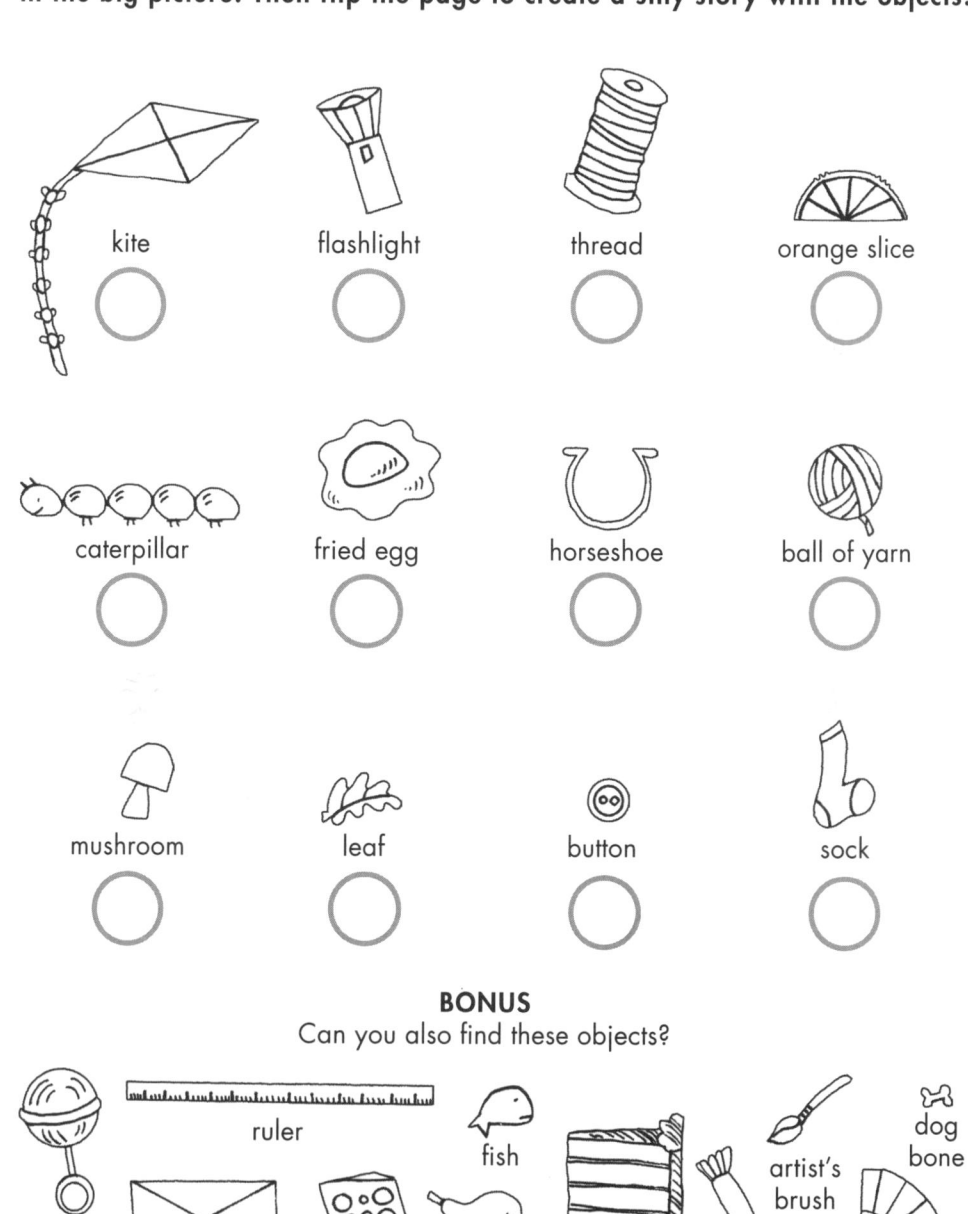

kite ◯

flashlight ◯

thread ◯

orange slice ◯

caterpillar ◯

fried egg ◯

horseshoe ◯

ball of yarn ◯

mushroom ◯

leaf ◯

button ◯

sock ◯

BONUS
Can you also find these objects?

ruler

fish

dog bone

baby's rattle

envelope

cheese

pear

cake

artist's brush

carrot

fan

First Day Jitters

Illustrated by Mernie Gallagher-Cole

Flip the page!

First Day Jitters

Write the object names in the numbered spaces. For example, if you found the horseshoe first, write "horseshoe" in the first blank.

When I woke up this morning, my _____

1

hurt and my _____ was all sweaty.

2

At first, I thought I must have eaten a weird

_____ with dinner last night. But then I

3

remembered: it was the first day at my new school,

_____ Elementary. Mom and Dad

4

made a big deal about it. Dad cooked his famous

bacon-covered _____ for breakfast, and

5

Mom gave me a new _____ to hang

6

on my backpack. That helped a little. But I was still

On Track

Illustrated by Dave Klug

Flip the page!

On Track

Write the object names in the numbered spaces. For example, if you found the shoe first, write "shoe" in the first blank.

Ever since I was a little _____, I have
1

loved to run. Nothing's better than feeling the

wind on my _____ while watching
2

the _____ zoom by. So I was as
3

excited as a wild _____ when Coach
4

_____ told me I made the track team.
5

But then he said I would need to try jumping over

a _____. That sounded harder than
6

running up a mountain with a _____ on
7

my head. I went to the first practice with butterflies in

my _____. At first, Coach took it easy

on me. I only had to jump over hurdles as tall as a

_____. That's when I learned that I could

run and jump at the same time. I practiced a lot. Dad

said I was turning into a bouncy _____!

But my hard work paid off. At my first track meet,

I ran the fastest in the _____. I think

my nervous butterflies helped me to fly down the

_____ and over each hurdle. What a

great feeling!

Hidden Pictures®

Write a number below each object based on the order in which you find it in the big picture. Then flip the page to create a silly story with the objects!

boot

bow tie

golf club

cupcake

fried egg

leaf

kite

sock

book

feather

sailboat

pie

BONUS
Can you also find these objects?

flag bowl tack candle banana mushroom hockey stick

Dog School

Flip the page!

Dog School

Write the object names in the numbered spaces. For example, if you found the sock first, write "sock" in the first blank.

"Sit!" "Stay!" "_____ 1 !" Sure, we dogs

know all these basic commands. But at Ms. Trixie's

School for _____ 2 Dogs, we learn new

tricks every day. Today we learned that it is not all

right to chew a _____ 3 or scratch a

person's _____ 4 , but it is OK to shake

paws with a _____ 5 . That news totally

made my _____ 6 wag. In class, I sit

next to a pug named Charlie. He is very nice, but

he can't seem to tell his _____ 7 from his

_____! Ms. Trixie has been working extra
         8

hard with him. Today, after he fetched the squeaky-toy

_____ from the back of the room, she
         9

gave him a peanut-butter-covered _____.
                                          10

I hope I earn one of those tomorrow! For homework

tonight, we each need to bark at a _____
                                              11

once and sniff a _____ twice. I think I
                          12

can handle it!

Hidden Pictures®

Write a number below each object based on the order in which you find it in the big picture. Then flip the page to create a silly story with the objects!

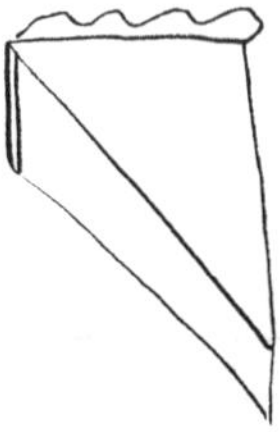

pie ○

kite ○

paintbrush ○

sock ○

sailboat ○

cupcake ○

horseshoe ○

butterfly ○

ice-cream cone ○

ring ○

pencil ○

toothbrush ○

BONUS
Can you also find these objects?

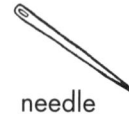 needle

 nail

 banana

 fork

Whee!

Flip the page!

Whee!

Write the object names in the numbered spaces. For example, if you found the kite first, write "kite" in the first blank.

The last day of school at _____ Academy
1

is always extra fun. Our whole _____
2

closes early and we all head to the big amusement

park. Our park has the best roller coasters

around—there's the Flying _____,
3

the _____ Plunge, and you won't
4

catch me missing out on my favorite, the Twisting

_____. If I had my way, I'd ride that
5

one all day long. But my friends like to go to the

_____ House. That's fun too, and
6

a little scary. When you walk through it, a giant

_____ jumps out at you, then you
    7

slide along a slimy _____ and land
                         8

in a big sticky _____. When we need
                      9

a break, we sit in the shade and lick a refreshing

frozen _____. Sometimes a friendly
            10

_____ in costume walks by and tries
     11

to make us laugh. Then we head to the biggest

_____ in the park and wait in a long line
     12

to ride it. By the end of the day, we're happy-tired and

already looking forward to next year's visit.

Hidden Pictures®

Write a number below each object based on the order in which you find it in the big picture. Then flip the page to create a silly story with the objects!

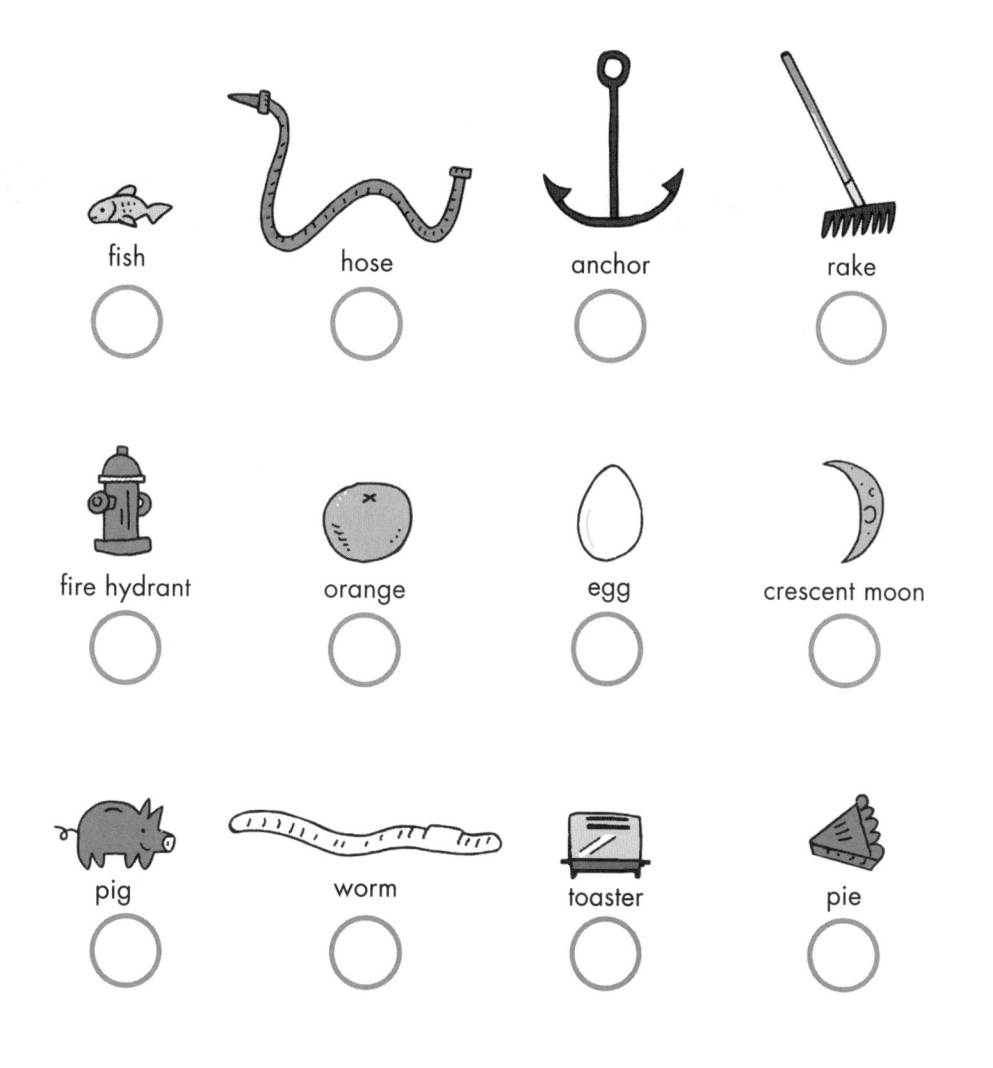

fish

hose

anchor

rake

fire hydrant

orange

egg

crescent moon

pig

worm

toaster

pie

Play Right

Illustrated by Dave Klug

Flip the page!

Play Right

Write the object names in the numbered spaces. For example, if you found the pig first, write "pig" in the first blank.

"This stage is our stage, this stage is your

_____!" We sang that at the start
       1

of our class play tonight. It took place on the

big _____ in the world-famous
       2

_____ Auditorium. The story features
      3

a wizard, a knight, and a princess. I played the

brave _____ in search of his lost
       4

_____. My best friend, Andrea, got to
     5

play a purple snow-covered _____!
                         6

Isn't that cool? In the play, I traveled to the distant

city of _____ 7 . There I found a beautiful

_____ 8 in a castle. She was in trouble.

She was about to be eaten by a terrible, fire-breathing

_____ 9 ! But don't worry. I came to her

rescue, just like any brave _____ 10 in

shining armor would. And I got help from a powerful

_____ 11 , who could cast spells. Together

we saved her and a precious _____ 12 from

her family's treasure chest. The whole cast grabbed

hands and bowed. The end!

Hidden Pictures®

Write a number below each object based on the order in which you find it in the big picture. Then flip the page to create a silly story with the objects!

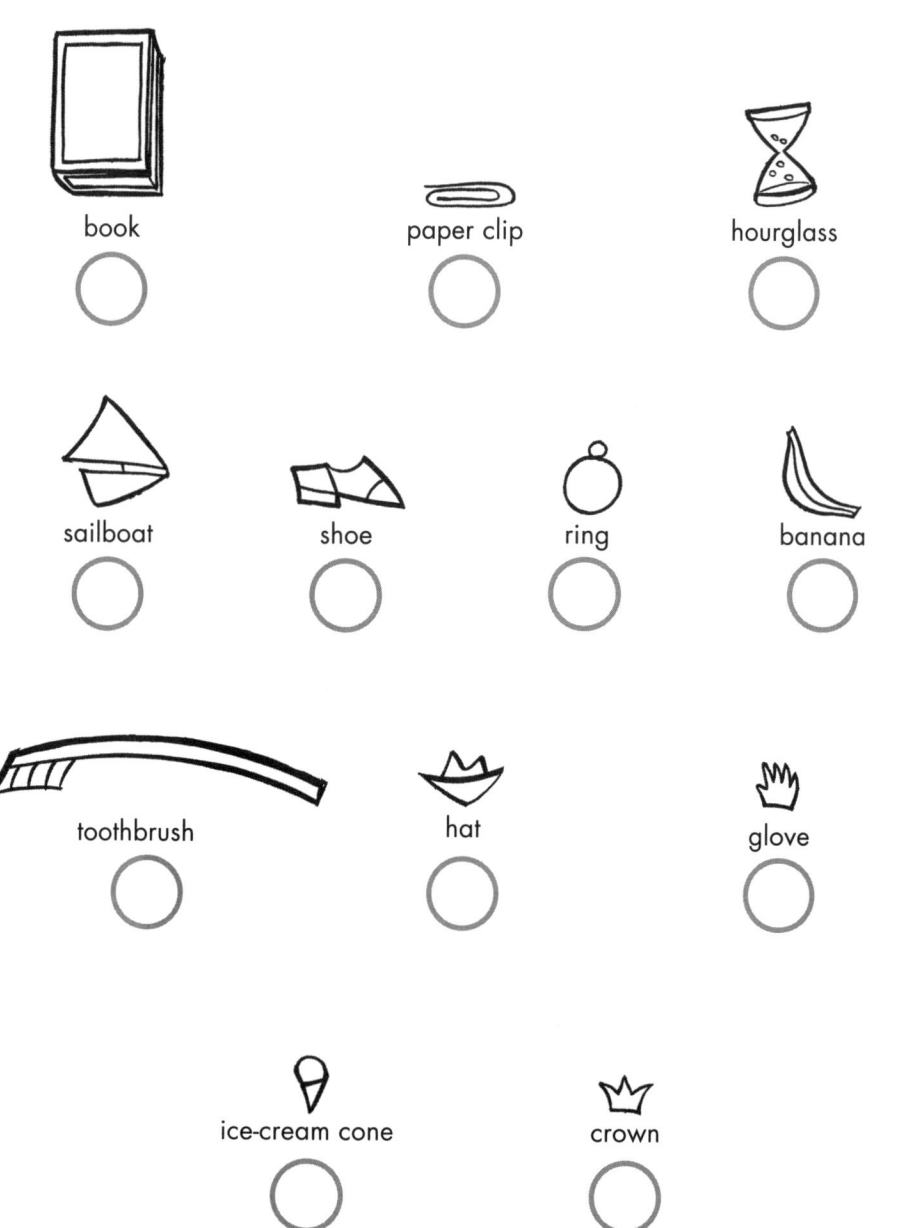

book

paper clip

hourglass

sailboat

shoe

ring

banana

toothbrush

hat

glove

ice-cream cone

crown

Lunchtime

Illustrated by Tim Davis

Flip the page!

27

Lunchtime

Write the object names in the numbered spaces. For example, if you found the sailboat first, write "sailboat" in the first blank.

I like everything about school. From my favorite

_____ class to playing on the
　　　1

_____ at recess, it's all super cool.
　　　2

But my favorite part is lunch. My best friend,

Bubbles _____ , and I always sit at the
　　　　　　　3

_____ table. That's the one right near the
　　　4

_____ counter. We usually pack our own
　　　5

_____ to eat, but we each buy a carton
　　　6

of foamy _____ to drink. That sure tastes
　　　　　7

good on a hot day! Today, a big, scary-looking

_____ swam up to our table. My fins
8

were shaking! I was afraid he wanted to take a bite

out of my favorite _____. Thankfully,
9

he just wanted to borrow a soft _____
10

to wipe his gills with. We had some extras, so we

were happy to share. He was polite and said,

"_____ you very much." We invited him
11

to sit with us, and he told tons of funny jokes, like this

one: "How did the fish cross the _____?
12

Very e-*fish*-iently!" School rules!

Hidden Pictures®

Write a number below each object based on the order in which you find it in the big picture. Then flip the page to create a silly story with the objects!

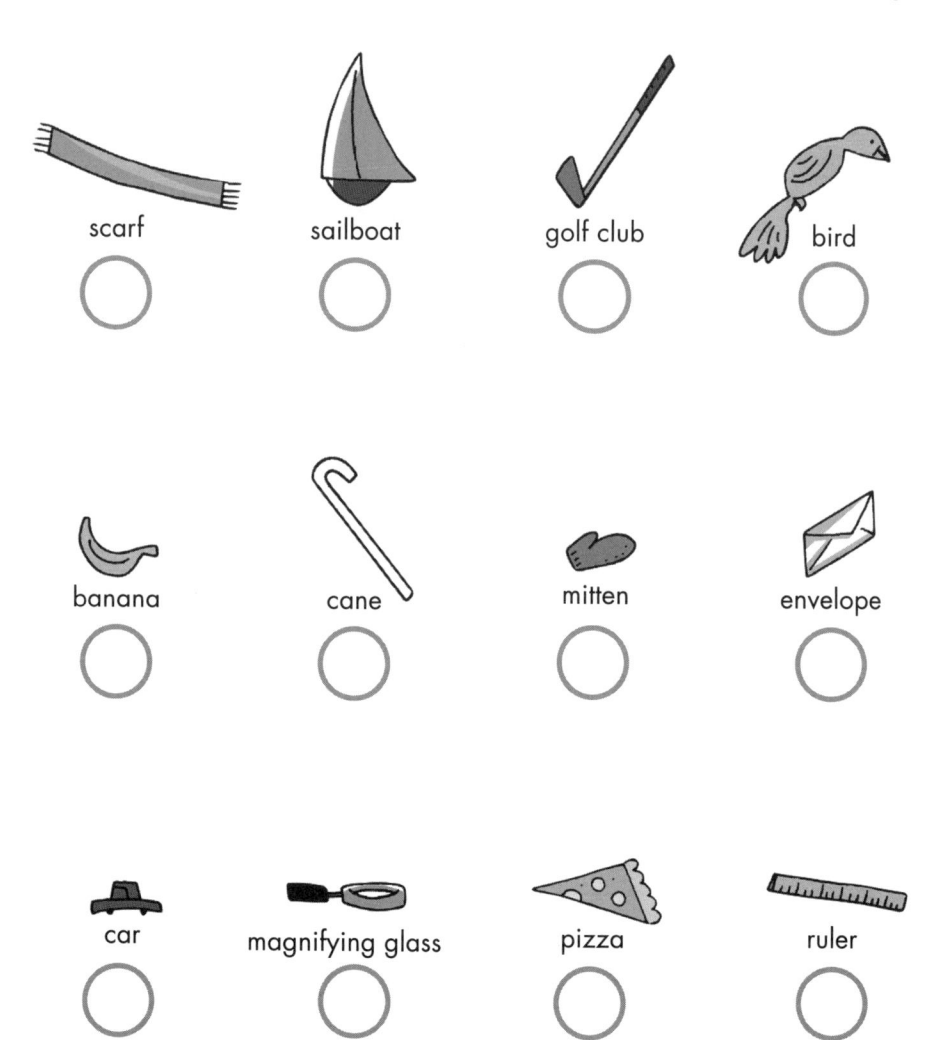

scarf
○

sailboat
○

golf club
○

bird
○

banana
○

cane
○

mitten
○

envelope
○

car
○

magnifying glass
○

pizza
○

ruler
○

Weird Science

Illustrated by Dave Klug

Flip the page!

Weird Science

Write the object names in the numbered spaces. For example, if you found the banana first, write "banana" in the first blank.

Today was the school _____ fair, and I

1

was so excited to reveal the project I'd been working

on for months: my robotic _____ 2000—

2

Robo for short. I had some finishing touches to make.

All I had left to do was tighten the _____

3

and wind up the _____ on the left

4

side of his head and he'd be ready. But right then,

something strange happened. My friend Abbey's pet

_____ went running by. All of a sudden

5

Robo seemed to have a _____ of his

6

own. He set his _____ in motion and

 7

rolled off. "Stop, Robo!" I called. I pressed the green

_____ on my remote, but Robo kept on

 8

rolling. He bumped into a _____, and

 9

then he ran over my teacher's _____.

 10

When he crossed the room, I thought he was about to

run right into a _____. Ouch! But, to the

 11

amazement of the whole room, he caught Abbey's pet

and saved the _____. Go Robo!

 12

Hidden Pictures®

Write a number below each object based on the order in which you find it in the big picture. Then flip the page to create a silly story with the objects!

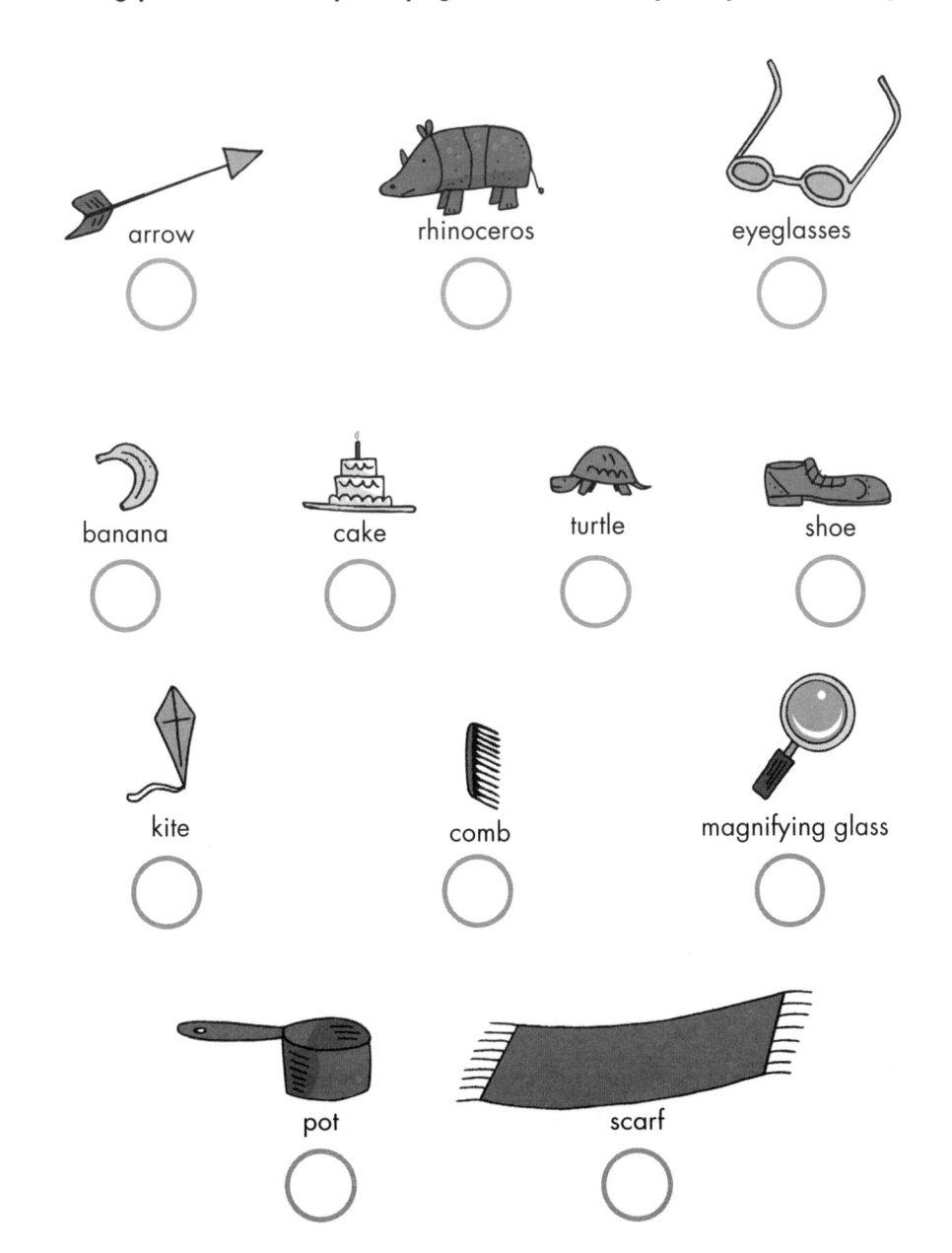

arrow

rhinoceros

eyeglasses

banana

cake

turtle

shoe

kite

comb

magnifying glass

pot

scarf

Sea Sights

Illustrated by Dave Klug

Flip the page!

S a Sights

Write the object names in the numbered spaces. For example, if you found the turtle first, write "turtle" in the first blank.

Yesterday, our class took a field trip to the ocean.

I climbed to the very tippy-top of a striped

_____. By the time I got to the last stair,
 1

I was hotter than a melting _____, but
 2

it was worth it. The view from the top was incredible!

I could see a sailing _____, a flying
 3

_____, and a blue _____
 4 5

that was squirting water. But then I saw someting

rolling across the sky. It was a big, dark

_____, and it was coming fast! Before
 6

you could say, "_____!" the rain started
                        7

to pour and my friends and I were soaked to the

_____. Ms. _____, our
        8   9

teacher, led us down the stairs and back onto the

school _____. We waited there for the
              10

storm to roll on by. The bus driver gave us each a

juice box and a delicious _____ to eat.
                                  11

As I was about to take my last bite, the sky cleared,

and just like that, the _____ was shining.
                              12

We all raced off the bus and down to the ocean. That

shore was a fun trip!

Hidden Pictures®

Write a number below each object based on the order in which you find it in the big picture. Then flip the page to create a silly story with the objects!

pie ◯

book ◯

drinking glass ◯

hanger ◯

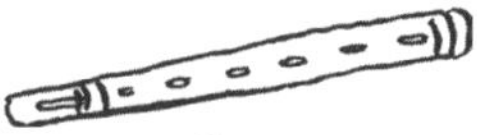

flute ◯

hat ◯

jug ◯

fish ◯

wristwatch ◯

lemon ◯

lightning bolt ◯

bowl ◯

BONUS
Can you also find these objects?

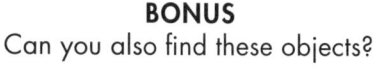

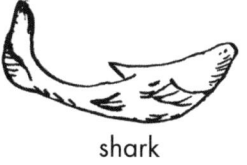 shark

 bird

Flying Frogs?!

Illustrated by Diana Zourelias

Flip the page!

Flying Frogs?!

Write the object names in the numbered spaces. For example, if you found the lemon first, write "lemon" in the first blank.

Frogs can't fly, right? That's what I used to think. But

not anymore. It all started months ago when Ms.

Biddle, our _____ teacher, brought
1

in a _____ full of tadpoles. We were
2

going to watch them grow and take notes on a

_____ for science class. Soon, our
3

_____ was stuffed with full-grown frogs,
4

and we had plenty of notes. It was time to take them

back where they belonged: to a _____
5

with plenty of fresh _____ to eat. So
6

we opened the top of the _____. One
                                    7

frog looked out. It flapped its _____
                                          8

and twirled its green _____, and before
                              9

anyone could say, "_____!" the frog was
                            10

flying across the room! Another joined in. The frogs

were everywhere—even on top of Ms. Biddle's head!

One by one they flew over the _____
                                        11

and out the open _____. I sure do
                          12

wonder where Ms. Biddle found those tadpoles!

Hidden Pictures ®

Write a number below each object based on the order in which you find it in the big picture. Then flip the page to create a silly story with the objects!

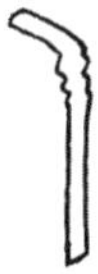

straw
◯

boot
◯

acorn
◯

crescent moon
◯

bowl
◯

hammer
◯

flashlight
◯

light bulb
◯

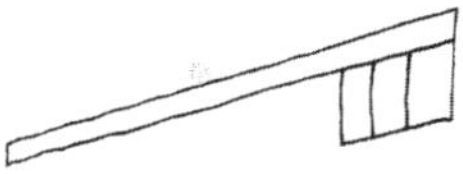

toothbrush
◯

pizza
◯

sailboat
◯

mug
◯

BONUS
Can you also find these objects?

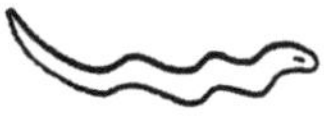

 snake    banana   heart

Hula Hoopla

Illustrated by Chuck Dillon

Flip the page!

Hula Hoopla

Write the object names in the numbered spaces. For example, if you found the pizza first, write "pizza" in the first blank.

Yesterday during _____ class at school,
1

Mr. Lang surprised us all by pulling some hula hoops

out of the storage _____. I had not
2

tried to spin a hoop around my _____
3

since I was knee-high to a _____. But
4

I guess it's like riding a _____ because
5

my body remembered exactly what to do. It was all

fun until my _____ bumped into Justin's.
6

Oops! He grabbed his _____, hopped
7

onto a _____, and glared at me. I felt
8

really bad and said I was sorry. Suddenly, a stray

_____ ran into the school yard and ran
          9

under all of our feet! Mr. Lang tried to lure it away

with a handful of _____ nuggets. But that
                              10

didn't work. It hopped right up to me, so I snapped my

fingers and said, "_____!" That made it
                              11

lie on its _____ and spin in circles, just
                    12

like a hula hoop. We all laughed, even Justin. Then we

spun again, too.

Hidden Pictures®

Write a number below each object based on the order in which you find it in the big picture. Then flip the page to create a silly story with the objects!

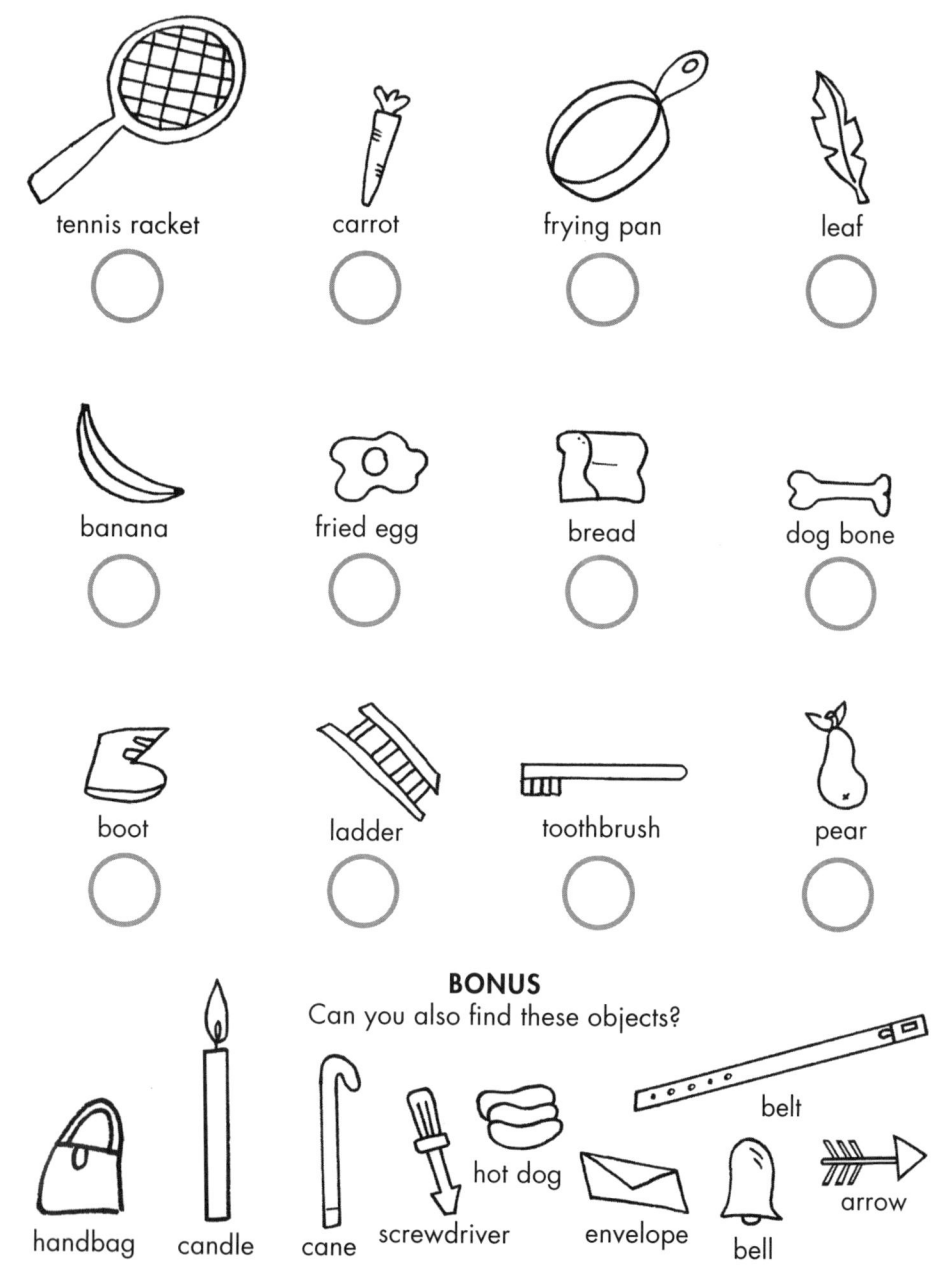

tennis racket ◯

carrot ◯

frying pan ◯

leaf ◯

banana ◯

fried egg ◯

bread ◯

dog bone ◯

boot ◯

ladder ◯

toothbrush ◯

pear ◯

BONUS
Can you also find these objects?

handbag

candle

cane

screwdriver

hot dog

belt

envelope

bell

arrow

Dreamy Art

Flip the page!

Dreamy Art

Write the object names in the numbered spaces. For example, if you found the banana first, write "banana" in the first blank.

Today's art class was highly unusual. First, our

teacher gave us each a piece of _____
                                              1

and told us to draw on it with a fine-tipped

_____. Then she told us to dip it in
        2

a pot of _____ and hang it on the
                  3

_____ to dry. Mine looked like a
        4

_____ that had stayed in the pool too long.
        5

Next, each of us had to pick one _____
                                                6

and glue a sparkly _____ to the back.
                          7

I couldn't help but wonder what our teacher was

up to! Then she said, "Class, I need you to each

pass your _____ to the student on
             8

your right. When you get your new one, fold it into

the shape of a _____, take it home,
                      9

and put it under your softest _____ as
                                        10

you sleep tonight." Now I understood! Our teacher

wanted us to dream up an idea for a new piece of

_____ that we could hang next to our
        11

damp art from today. I couldn't wait to see what my

dream _____ looked like!
            12

Hidden Pictures®

Write a number below each object based on the order in which you find it in the big picture. Then flip the page to create a silly story with the objects!

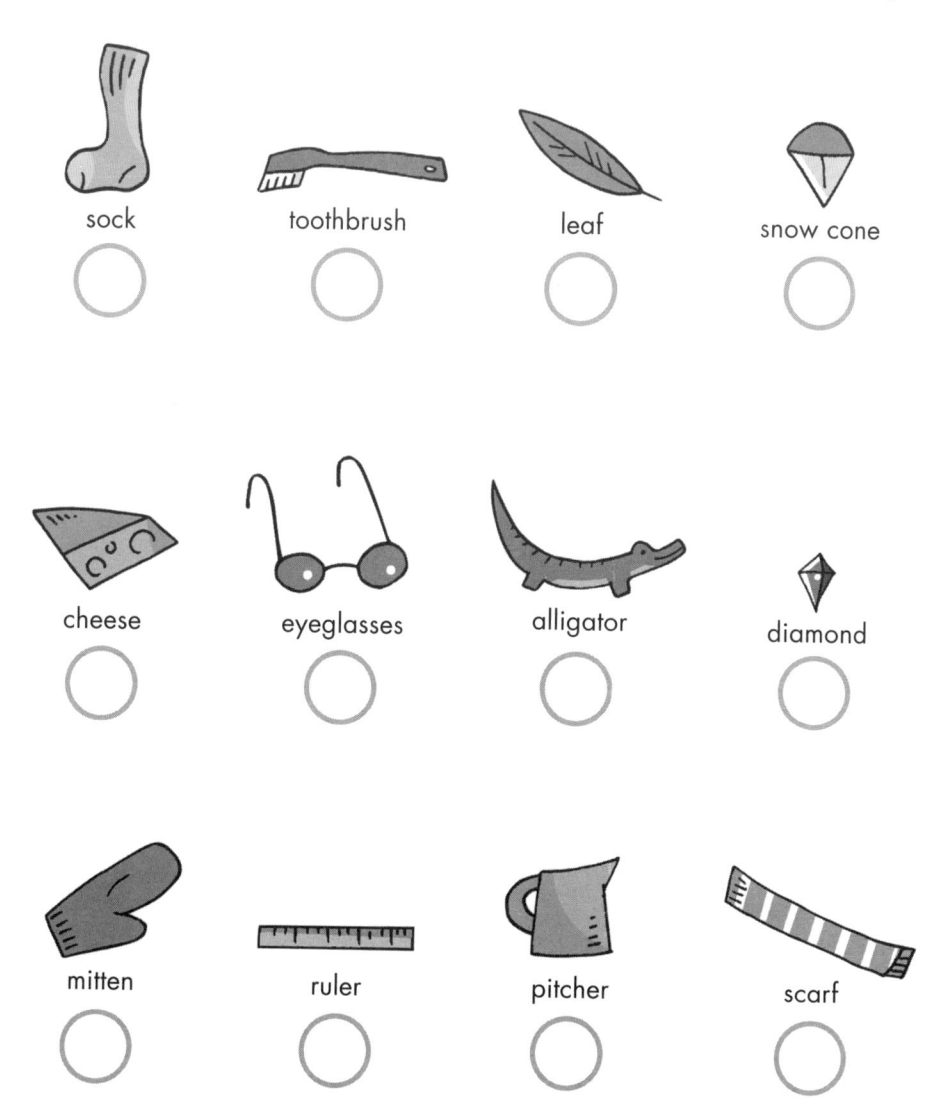

sock

toothbrush

leaf

snow cone

cheese

eyeglasses

alligator

diamond

mitten

ruler

pitcher

scarf

Flutterby Fans

Illustrated by Dave Klug

Flip the page!

Flutterby Fans

Write the object names in the numbered spaces. For example, if you found the mitten first, write "mitten" in the first blank.

Our town's _____ museum just opened

1

a cool new exhibit: a big _____ full

2

of butterflies! My class took a trip there today. It

was so crowded that we had to stand in a long

_____ before we could go in. But it was

3

worth the wait! At first, it seemed like there wasn't a

single _____ in sight. But then I realized

4

that they were everywhere. I saw a giant yellow

_____, a tiny spotted _____,

5   6

and a pink-and-white-striped _____.

7

My best friend, Tony, had a friendly little

_____ land on his shoulder!
          8

Our teacher snapped a picture of us with his

_____ and said he would put it in
          9

the school's _____. My mom and my
                        10

_____ sure are going to be excited to
          11

see that. Speaking of my parents, I'm going to ask

them to bring me back to the _____ this
                                              12

weekend. I can't wait!

Hidden Pictures®

Write a number below each object based on the order in which you find it in the big picture. Then flip the page to create a silly story with the objects!

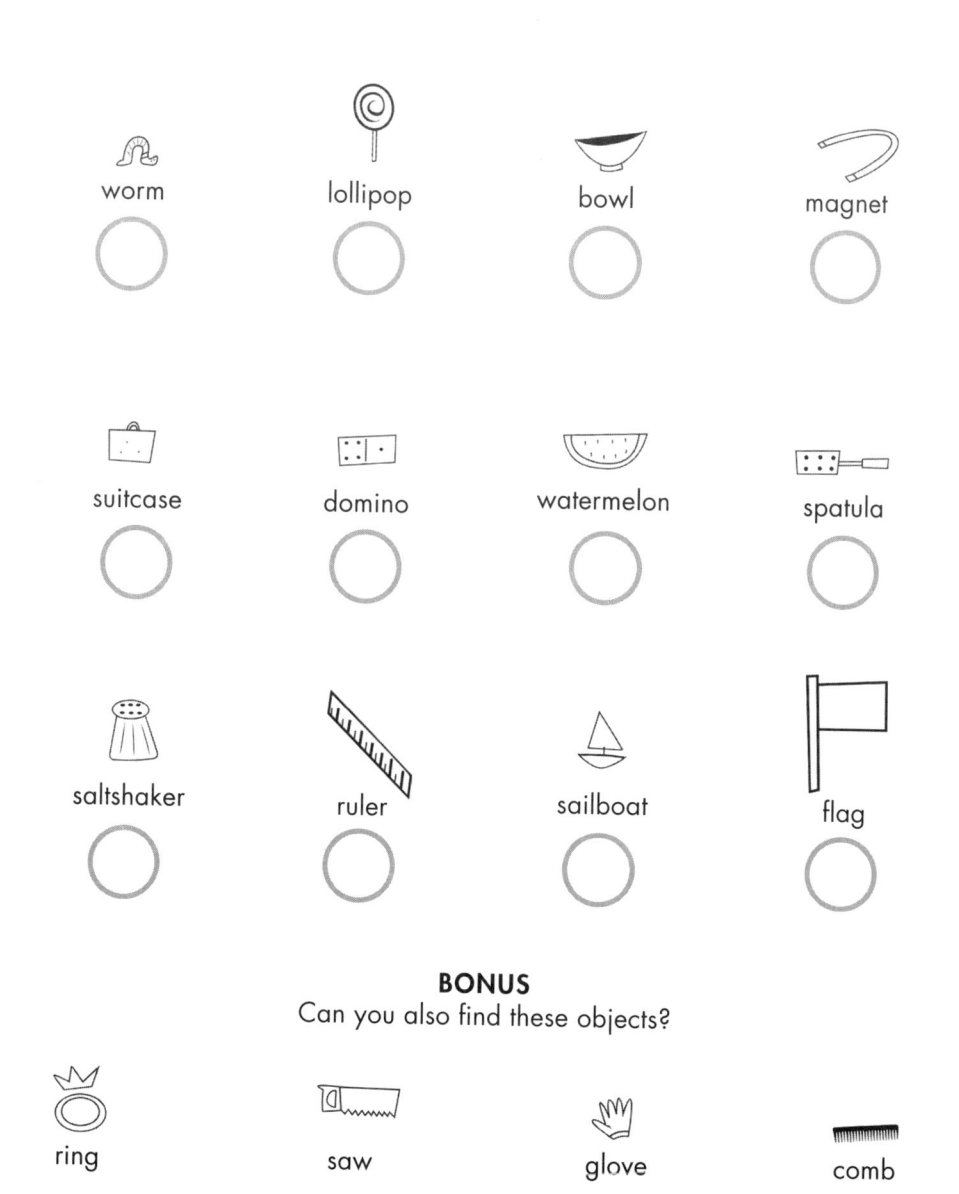

worm ◯

lollipop ◯

bowl ◯

magnet ◯

suitcase ◯

domino ◯

watermelon ◯

spatula ◯

saltshaker ◯

ruler ◯

sailboat ◯

flag ◯

BONUS
Can you also find these objects?

ring

saw

glove

comb

Fresh Baked

Illustrated by Mike Moran

Flip the page!

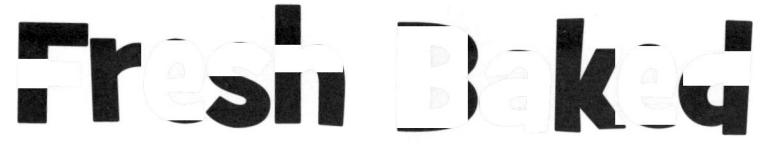

Fresh Baked

Write the object names in the numbered spaces. For example, if you found the lollipop first, write "lollipop" in the first blank.

Every fall, our school holds a _____

1

sale as a fundraiser. This year, we are raising

money so that the sixth grade can travel on a

_____ to go to the _____

2   3

Museum. It's an expensive trip, so we need to sell

every single _____ that we can. Last

4

night, my mom helped me bake my favorite treat:

_____ cookies with _____

5   6

chips. Delicious! My best friend Maddie made her

famous blueberry _____ muffins, and our

7

teacher brought Crunchy _____ Nuggets.
8

In addition to desserts, people donated veggies

and fruits from their own gardens. I sold a crunchy

green _____ to my dad and a spicy red
9

_____ to my neighbor. At the end of
10

the day, our principal announced that we had raised

enough money to go on our _____ trip.
11

"_____!" yelled Maddie. I couldn't have
12

said it better myself.

Hidden Pictures®

Write a number below each object based on the order in which you find it in the big picture. Then flip the page to create a silly story with the objects!

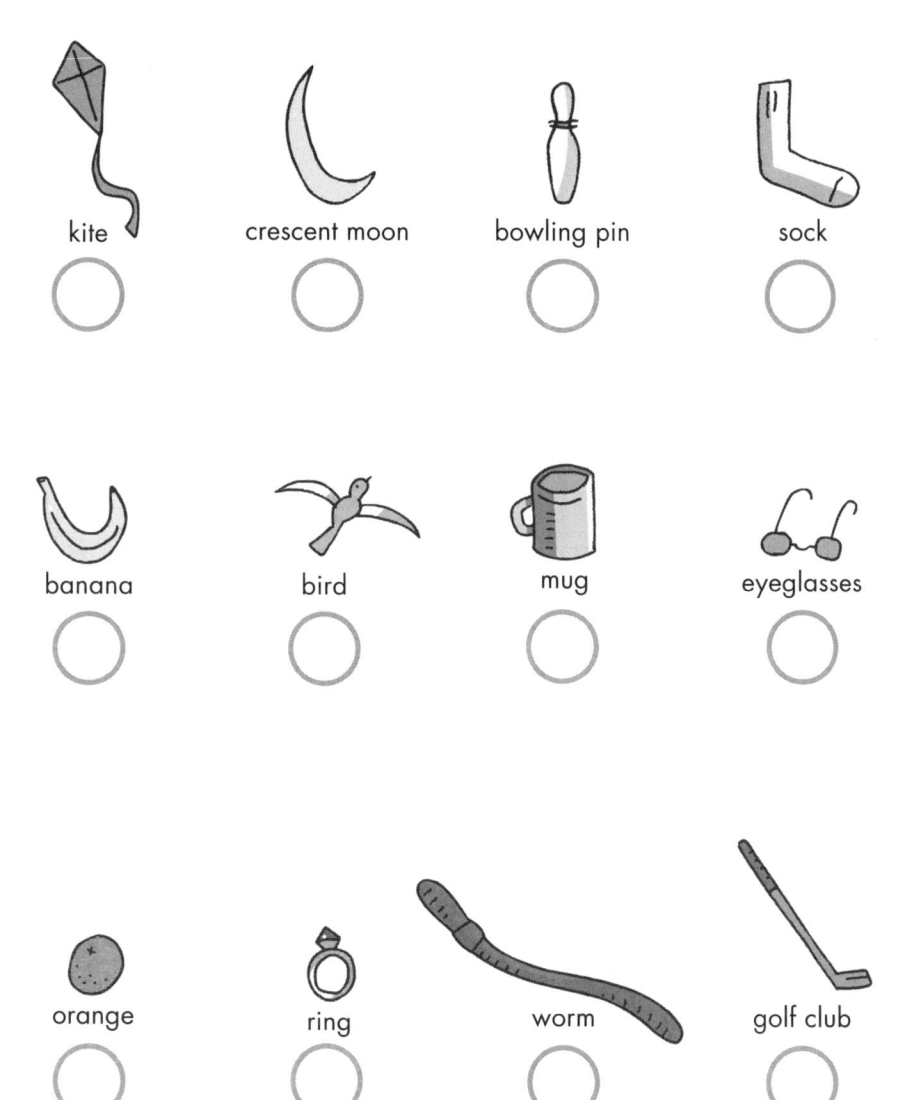

kite

crescent moon

bowling pin

sock

banana

bird

mug

eyeglasses

orange

ring

worm

golf club

Keep the Beat

Illustrated by Dave Klug

Flip the page!

Keep the Beat

Write the object names in the numbered spaces. For example, if you found the eyeglasses first, write "eyeglasses" in the first blank.

My school band rocks. For real! For our concert, we

are playing "Rock around the _____,"
                                    1

"_____ Rock," and "Shake Your
        2

_____!" Our band director used
        3

to play drums in the famous band The Purple

_____, so she knows all about
        4

_____ music. We've been practicing
        5

since the start of the scool year, so I can't wait for

each _____ in our families to hear
            6

our spectacular songs. Once we were all set up on

stage, the curtain rose. But as we played the first

_____, we all knew that something was
        7

wrong. We couldn't hear the big _____
                                         8

drum. Our drummer Joey _____
                              9

was missing! "Stay calm," the director mouthed

to us. "Keep playing." We tried, but first Katie's

_____ squeaked, and then my
        10

_____ fell off my music stand. Oh no!
        11

Just then, Joey ran on stage. He'd been stuck in the

band's _____ room. Finally we were
        12

back in rhythm. It rocked!

Answers

Page 1

There are 4 slices of pizza, 2 hot dogs, 3 cupcakes, and 8 bananas hidden in this pad.

There are the most rulers hidden (4).

3 Bagpipe Concert

7 First Day Jitters

11 On Track

15 Dog School

19 Whee!

Answers

23 Play Right

27 Lunchtime

31 Weird Science

35 Sea Sights

39 Flying Frogs?!

43 Hula Hoopla

Answers

47 Dreamy Art

55 Fresh Baked

51 Flutterby Fans

59 Keep the Beat